Contents

To my partner Simon,

who made the time to work through my first draft

but sadly did not live to see it in print.

My best friend, I'll love you always

Flora

Chapter 1
What is Dreamweaver?

Dreamweaver is a web authoring tool used to create web pages. As you may or may not know, the code used to write web pages is called HTML (HyperText Markup Language). Before the days of packages such as Dreamweaver, people used to create web pages purely by writing HTML code – if you wanted a particular image to appear on a page, you couldn't just insert the image in the right place, you had to write the code to position it and to retrieve the correct image file. You'll be relieved to hear that with Dreamweaver, all you do is insert the image wherever you want on a page – in about three mouse clicks.

Web pages are still coded in HTML, but you don't even have to know it exists, because you just tell Dreamweaver in simple terms how you want the web page to look, and it writes all the HTML for you! Dreamweaver is called a WYSIWYG program, short for What You See is What You Get, for the simple reason that Dreamweaver always shows you an accurate picture of what the final web page will look like. It is advisable as you become more familiar with Dreamweaver to learn how HTML works (this is mainly useful for debugging, if for some reason Dreamweaver doesn't do what you want it to), but to begin with you can get away with ignoring it completely.

Getting Dreamweaver

If you don't already have Dreamweaver installed, you can purchase a copy from their web site www.dreamweaver.com, or alternatively download a free fully working 30-day trial version. Full instructions on how to buy or trial the package are on the web site.

Additional Software

Dreamweaver is produced by Macromedia who produce several other software programs for web developers such as Flash and Fireworks. This book does not assume you have any of these additional programs.

It is nice when developing web pages to be able to create your own simple graphics, if only to create smart-looking buttons and menus. You don't need a graphics package to work through this book because you can download all the graphics used from the Payne-Gallway web site (you'll be talked through this later). If you do want to have a go at designing your own graphics, one of the simplest and cheapest graphics packages is Paint Shop Pro – that's what was used to create the graphics you'll download later.

Tip:
A **web site** is a collection of **web pages**, linked together by a menu system. In this book you will build a complete web site by creating the web pages individually and then linking them together.

Tip:
If you want to learn more about Paint Shop Pro, look at **Basic Paint Shop Pro** by R. Chasemore – visit **www.payne-gallway.co.uk** for details.

The Alpe Retreats web site

Throughout this book you will create and develop a web site for a company called **Alpe Retreats**. Alpe Retreats is a small company that owns and runs four chalets in Val Thorens in the French Alps. They need a web site so that anyone looking for a chalet in Val Thorens can look up the details and prices. They would also like customers to be able to view the availability of the chalets and fill in a provisional booking form on the web site that is then e-mailed to the company.

The first step when creating any web page is to get a good picture in your mind of what you want the web site to look like and what it needs to contain. You should plan it out on paper before jumping onto the computer.

A rough plan of the pages that will make up the Alpe Retreats web site is shown below. There are six links on the left of each page that, when clicked, will take the user to the relevant page. Notice that the menu (also called a **navigation bar**) and the title are the same on every page.

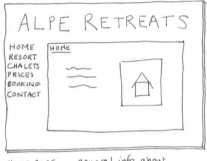

HOME PAGE — general info about Alpe Retreats + photo of a chalet.

RESORT PAGE — general info about Val Thorens.

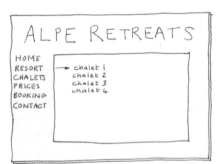

A second chalets menu appears when cursor is on CHALETS link. User can click on chalet name to view chalet details.

ALPE RETREATS

HOME
RESORT
CHALETS
PRICES
BOOKING
CONTACT

CHALETS > chalet 3

CHALETS > chalet 3 PAGE — info and
photo of chalet.

ALPE RETREATS

HOME
RESORT
CHALETS
PRICES
BOOKING
CONTACT

PRICES

Date	Chalet 1	Chalet 2	...

PRICES PAGE — list of dates + prices
for all chalets

ALPE RETREATS

HOME
RESORT
CHALETS
PRICES
BOOKING
CONTACT

BOOKING

Name
Address

Date
Chalet

SUBMIT

BOOKING PAGE — user will fill out
a booking form which
is then emailed to
Alpe Retreats.

ALPE RETREATS

HOME
RESORT
CHALETS
PRICES
BOOKING
CONTACT

CONTACT

Address

Phone
email

Chapter 2
Creating a New Web Site

In this chapter we will create the Alpe Retreats web site. You'll learn how to define a site and set up a good file structure for the whole site.

 Load Dreamweaver. You can do this in one of two ways:

 Either double-click the Dreamweaver icon on your windows desktop

 Or click Start, Programs then find the Macromedia folder and select Dreamweaver.

If this is the first time you have opened Dreamweaver, it will ask you about workspace options. Basically, you get a choice between how the old version of Dreamweaver looked, and the new Dreamweaver MX version:

Figure 2.1: The Workspace Setup window

▶ Choose the Dreamweaver MX Workspace by making sure the first option button is selected and then clicking OK.

Don't worry if you've selected the wrong option! You can correct it using the Preferences window as shown below.

▶ Select Edit, Preferences from the menu bar at the top of the screen.

The Preferences window appears.

▶ Select General from the left-hand list of categories then click the Change Workspace button. This will open the window shown in Figure 2.1 above.

Figure 2.2: Preferences

▶ Click OK to close the Preferences window.

Folder structure

When you set up a new site, you will be asked where on your computer you want it to be saved. It is therefore a good idea to create a suitable folder structure before opening a new site.

Each page on your site and each image you use will be a separate file. By the time you've created a web site with many pages and images there will be a lot of files, so you need to make sure they are well-organised from the start.

For any web site, the main folders you will want are:

HTML files

Each page in your web site will be an HTML file, and will go in this folder.

Images

Any image inserted on a web page is stored separately as an image file, and should be put in this folder. The image files used in the Alpe Retreats web site are all JPEG (.jpg) files; other common file types used for images are .gif and .png.

Library

The library is not actually used in this book but we'll create the folder anyway because it is good practice.

When you are creating your web site, you can add various objects such as images or paragraphs of text to the library. This is useful for items that are used often, because if a library item is updated, every instance of this library item is also updated. Each item added to the library is given its own library file, which is stored in this folder.

Templates

As soon as you create a template, Dreamweaver will automatically create the Templates folder for you, so you won't need to create that. You can create templates in Dreamweaver in much the same way as Word. Once the template is created, you can base subsequent pages on that template. All template files have the file extension .dwt and will be stored in this folder.

Creating the folders

You can create the folders using the Site panel in Dreamweaver. However, if you are completely new to Dreamweaver it may be advisable to use Windows Explorer because you will be more familiar with it. We'll use the Site panel later.

Using Windows Explorer

To create the folders in Windows Explorer.

Open Windows Explorer by right-clicking on the Start button and clicking Explore from the context menu that appears.

Find a suitable place to put the web site folders; this will probably be somewhere in My Documents.

Create a folder and name it Alpe Retreats Website.

Create three more folders in the Alpe Retreats Website folder named HTML_files, Images and Library. You don't need to create the Templates folder yet because Dreamweaver will create it for you when you save your first template.

Your file structure should now look like this:

Figure 2.3: The file structure

Close Explorer and return to Dreamweaver.

Using the Site panel

In Dreamweaver, click the Site panel in the Files panel group.

If you have already created your folders, you should be able to navigate to them in just the same way you would in Explorer. If you haven't created them yet, navigate to where you want the root folder of the site to be located and use the commands on the File menu in the Site panel to create the folders.

Creating a new site

▶ On the main menu bar in Dreamweaver, select Site, New Site….

Figure 2.4: The Site menu

The Site Definition window appears. By default the Basic tab will be selected. This will take you through the Wizard. We will not use the wizard, as it includes a lot of options that we just don't need at this stage.

▶ Click the Advanced tab.

Figure 2.5: Site Definition

▶ Enter Alpe Retreats as the name for the web site.

 ▶ Click the Browse icon next to the Local Root Folder field and locate the folder Alpe Retreats Website you just created.

Figure 2.6: Selecting a local root folder for the site

Click Select.

You don't need to fill in any of the other options just yet, so just click OK.

 If you want to change any of the options you've just set, go to Site, Edit Sites… on the main menu bar. The Edit Sites dialogue box will appear; select the Alpe Retreats site and click the Edit button.

All done! You've set up the Alpe Retreats site.

Dreamweaver automatically creates a new blank page and calls it untitled-1

Figure 2.7: The Dreamweaver MX workspace with a blank pageblank page

 If the Untitled-1 page doesn't take up the whole window as shown in the screenshot above, click the Maximise icon (shown right) at the top right of the window.

Your screen should now look like the one above. Rather than introducing all the different parts of the workspace now, we'll just cover a few basics here and then the rest as you need them.

Panels

Many of the useful commands in Dreamweaver are contained in panels. Panels are very similar to windows which you will have come across in other applications. They can be hidden, minimised or closed in a similar way to windows. The panels are located to the right of the workspace – there are about six panel groups in that list (Design, Code, Application, Files, Advanced Layout and Answers). Don't worry – you don't need to know about most of these right now, in fact in this book you'll only need to use about half of them.

Tip:
If your site doesn't appear in the Site panel, select Alpe Retreats from the first menu in the Site panel and Local view from the second menu

Tip:
You may prefer to work without a grid (as shown in the screenshot). If a grid appears on your page, select View, Grid, Show Grid.

11

Showing and hiding panels

If you are missing any of the panels shown in the screenshot above, follow the steps below to add them to your workspace. You don't need to do this now – you can wait until you need to use a particular panel if you like.

▶ Select Window from the main menu bar.

ⓘ Some of the panels are grouped, for example the Site panel and the Assets panel are both in the Files panel group. If you open one of the panels in a group, the whole group will open.

▶ Only the names of the panels appear in the Window menu – not the panel groups. To open a panel click the name of the panel in the Window menu. It should then appear on the right of the screen with the other panels.

Figure 2.8: The Window menu

▶ To close a panel group, click the icon in the top right of the panel group, and select Close Panel Group from the menu.

Expanding and collapsing panel groups

The panel groups are designed so that you can expand and collapse them, depending on which one you are using at the time. In Figure 2.7 the Design and Files panel groups are expanded.

▶ To expand or collapse a panel, just click the small arrow next to the panel name.

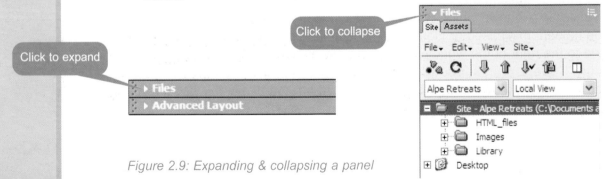

Figure 2.9: Expanding & collapsing a panel

Resizing panels

You can resize the width of the panels by clicking and dragging the grey border between the panel groups and the page.

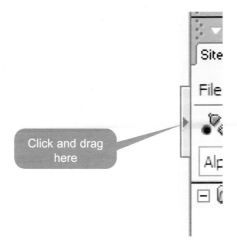

Figure 2.10: Widening panels

The Site panel

Notice that all the folders you have set up now appear in the Site panel under the Files panel group. Dreamweaver has inserted the text Site - Alpe Retreats where the folder name Alpe Retreats Website was (this is because Alpe Retreats was the name you gave to the site when setting up); the file pathname next to the text gives the original folder name.

If your folders don't appear in the Site panel, make sure you have Alpe Retreats and Local View selected as shown below:

Figure 2.11

You can easily change folder names, add new folders or delete files using the Site panel – you don't need to use Windows Explorer. All folders that are associated with a web site are coloured green; because you specified that the site would be stored in the Alpe Retreats Website folder, all folders within that folder will be associated with that web site and will be coloured green.

Saving a web page

All the pages you create for the Alpe Retreats web site will be based on a template that we will create in the next chapter. Here we'll create and save a web page that is not based on a template, just for practice. We'll then delete the page.

Let's save the blank page that is currently open (called Untitled-1) as test_page.

 From the top menu bar (not the one in the File panel), select File, Save As.

Figure 2.12: Saving a web page

The Save As dialogue box appears.

 We'll save it in the HTML_files folder, so double-click this. Now enter the file name test_page.html in the File name box.

Figure 2.13: Saving a web page

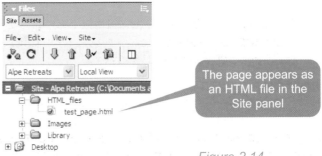 Notice that in the Save as type box it lists many different file extensions next to All Documents, not just one; this is fine. Click Save when your screen looks like the one above.

The page appears as an HTML file in the Site panel

Figure 2.14

In the Site panel, click the small plus symbol next to the HTML_files folder. You should now be able to see the test_page file. Notice that it has saved the file with a .html file extension.

The test_page file now represents one web page within your web site – although it is currently blank.

Deleting a web page

To delete a web page, all you do is delete its file. To avoid confusing error messages, it is best to make sure a file is closed before you try and delete it.

Closing a page

 Close the test_page by right-clicking on the sheet tab and selecting Close from the context menu that appears.

Figure 2.15: Closing a page

The page will disappear.

 If you wanted to open the page again, you would just double-click it in the Site panel.

 In the Site panel, click to select the test_page file. Now either press the Delete key or select File, Delete from the menu in the Site panel.

Figure 2.16: Deleting a page

 If you try to delete a page without closing it first, it will still remain open, and you will see messages saying you should resave it, and asking if you want to. If this happens, don't resave.

Deleting pages that are linked to other pages

If you try and delete a page that has links to it from another page, Dreamweaver will list the links to the site and ask for confirmation that you wish to delete the page.

Figure 2.17: Deleting a linked page

If you just agree to Dreamweaver's warnings it will delete the page OK. If you get a message about links, this means that when you delete the page, another page will contain a link that doesn't do anything! Open up the page(s) that Dreamweaver says contains the link and delete the link.

The Answers panel

The Dreamweaver help functions are in the Answers panel. If you can't see the Answers panel, select Window, Answers from the main menu bar.

If you need any extra help with anything, open up the Answers panel and click Tutorials. From here you have access to the Tutorials, as well as Help Contents, Search and Index.

If you need help on a particular subject, click the Search tab and enter the subject in the space at the top of the window. Click List Topics to see what help is available.

Figure 2.18: Getting help

When you have finished using the help functions, click the red Close icon.

Chapter 3
Creating a Template

You'll be pleased to hear that this is where the fun, creative bit starts. The key to a really professional-looking web site is to use a clean, simple template and to base every page on the same template. The navigation bar is also included on the template, so that whichever page you are on you have access to the same navigation buttons. This not only makes the web site look professional and coherent, it also makes it easy for people to browse your web site without getting lost!

You can have a lot of fun creating your own buttons and logos to use on this web site using a simple graphics package. However, if you don't want to learn a graphics package or you just don't have the time, the first thing you need to do is download all the images used in advance – if you download everything now, you'll have all the necessary images to hand for the rest of the book.

Downloading the image files

All the image files you need to create the Alpe Retreats web site can be downloaded from the Payne-Gallway web site.

Go to www.payne-gallway.co.uk/dreamweaver and follow the onscreen instructions.

Make sure you download the images into the Images folder that you set up in the last chapter. When you have downloaded them all, your file structure should look like this in the Site panel.

Figure 3.1: The Site panel after downloading the image files

Creating a new template

You can create a template from scratch or an existing page can be converted into a template. We'll create a basic page and then later save it as a template.

Tip:
You could create a template page by selecting **HTML Template** from the **Basic Page** list. This would achieve the same result as saving the basic page as a template.

 Select **File**, **New** from the main menu bar.

Figure 3.2: The New Document window

 Make sure **Basic Page** is selected in the **Category** list and **HTML** from the second list. Click **Create**.

Figure 3.3: The new blank page appears

Remember – you've opened a new page, but it is not yet saved. When a file is saved it will appear in the **Site** panel. We'll save the page now as a template.

▶ Select **File**, **Save as Template**… from the main menu bar.

Figure 3.4: Saving a page as a template

▶ Save the template as **main_template** and click **Save**.

The template may not yet be shown in the **Site** panel – you may need to refresh it first.

▶ In the **Site** panel, click the **Refresh** icon.

Figure 3.5: The main_template file appears in the Site panel

Although you didn't specify *where* Dreamweaver should save the file, it has automatically created a Templates folder and put it in there. If you had created the Templates folder along with the others, it would have found that and saved it in there.

Tables

You've probably come across tables in Microsoft Word where they are used to store data in columns and rows. Well, in Dreamweaver tables can be used to store columns and rows of data, but their main use is actually as a layout tool.

By using a large table, the size of the whole web page, you can adjust the columns and rows to divide up the page into sections.

A large table, the width of the whole page will be the basis of our template.

The Insert bar

Whenever you want to insert anything, whether it be a table, an image, a nav bar etc, you will use the Insert bar. This is located at the top of the screen, just below the main menu bar.

 If you can't see the Insert bar it may be hidden. Select Window, Insert from the main menu bar to open it.

If you want to know what any of the icons are on the Insert bar, just hold the mouse over the icon for a few seconds, and the Tool tip will appear with the name of the icon.

Inserting a table

▶ Make sure the cursor is in the top left of the page (it will be unless you've moved it), this is where we want to insert the table.

 ▶ Click the Insert Table icon on the Insert bar.

Figure 3.6: The Insert Table window

Fill out the **Insert Table** dialogue box as above, with **3** rows and **3** columns. Enter the width as **100%**. A value of 0 for the border gives an invisible border.

In Dreamweaver you can choose whether to size an object in **relative** or **absolute** terms. You can size an object **relative** to the size of the browser window by giving the size as a **percentage**. You can give an **absolute** size by specifying the number of **pixels**. It's difficult to gauge the size you want a table in pixels, so it is often easier to create a table as **100%**, resize it by eye, then convert all lengths to pixels. By specifying the sizes in pixels you can more easily cater for people with smaller screen sizes. We'll leave the sizes as percent for now; we'll cover how to change them to pixels later.

Click **OK**.

Figure 3.7: The new table appears at the top of the page

The table appears as shown above. It will need resizing but we'll do that in a minute.

Tip:
You can just enter a width in pixels if you know the size you want. Most sites use a width of about **800** pixels. At this size, each page of your site will fit onto most screens without users having to scroll across. Some sites are as narrow as **600** pixels – this means that even people with relatively small screens can view a page without scrolling, but you can't fit as much on a page. **www.payne-gallway.co.uk** uses a width of 600 pixels. **www.bbc.co.uk** uses just less than **800**.

Selecting cells, rows and tables

The table in the screenshot above is selected – as yours probably is because you've just created it. You can tell that it is selected because it has a solid black border and small black handles around it.

 Click away from the table to deselect it. The handles will disappear.

 Now click in the middle of the table. Look at the text just below the page tabs:

These are called tags, and the area they are in is called the Tag selector. Clicking on them here will select the objects they represent.

Clicking <td> will select the cell that the cursor is in.

Clicking <tr> will select the row the cursor is in.

Clicking <table> will select the table the cursor is in.

 Click each of these tags in turn and watch the black border highlight different parts of the table. This is the easiest way to select parts of a table.

The Properties inspector

At the bottom of the screen is the Properties inspector (it is essentially another panel, but Dreamweaver calls it an inspector not a panel). You can immediately view the properties of any object on the page just by selecting it.

 Select the table you've just created by clicking the <table> tag.

 If your Properties inspector is smaller than the one above you might need to expand yours. To do this, just click the small arrow in the bottom right of the Properties inspector.

The table properties appear in the Properties inspector. You'll learn more about these properties in a minute.

 Look at the properties of a cell and row by selecting them and viewing them in the Properties inspector.

Inserting and deleting rows and columns

Adding or deleting the last row or column

You can add or delete the bottom row or right-hand column simply by changing the number of rows and columns in the table properties (in the Properties inspector).

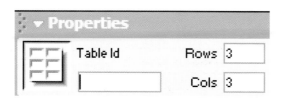

Make sure the table is selected. Change the number of rows to 4 and columns to 2 using the Properties inspector.

Another way to add a row is to place the cursor in the last cell in a table and press the Tab key.

Inserting or deleting a row or column in the middle of a table

Right-click in the top left cell in the table.

Figure 3.8: Inserting a column

Select Table, Insert Column from the context menu that appears.

The table should now have 3 columns.

Use the same method to delete one of the rows.

Merging and splitting cells

You can easily merge and split cells, so that the number of rows and columns varies across the table. The quickest way to merge and split cells is to use the icons in the Properties inspector.

Merging

▶ Select the entire second row in the table. Click the Merge Cells icon in the Properties inspector.

Figure 3.9: Merging cells

The cells are merged, and there's only one column in the second row.

Splitting

▶ Select the centre cell in row 3.

▶ Click the Split Cells icon in the Properties inspector.

Figure 3.10: Splitting cells

The Split Cell dialogue box appears. You have the choice of splitting the cell into rows or columns. You can also specify how many rows or columns.

▶ Enter the settings shown above, and then click OK.

Figure 3.11: Splitting cells

The cell is split in two horizontally.

Resizing cells and tables

Resizing a table

The table should at least fill the visible area on the screen, so we need to make it much longer.

 Select the whole table. Place the mouse over the bottom handle so that it becomes a small arrow.

Figure 3.12: Resizing a table

 Click and drag the handle down so that the table is about **1000** pixels (the height will be shown in the **Properties** inspector). Release the mouse when you're happy with the size.

Resizing cells

To resize cells, just click and drag the table border between the cells.

 Place the mouse over the border you want to resize so that the cursor becomes an arrow.

 Click and drag the border to where you want it, then release it.

 Click and drag the borders so that your table looks like the one below.

Tip:
You don't need to worry that a table cell won't be big enough to fit an object because the table will always grow to fit whatever you put in.

Converting the table widths to pixels

Now that the table is the right size, we'll convert the widths from % to pixels. Percentages are good if you want the template to resize according to how large a browser window is, but because people will be viewing your web site on different sized screens it is best to size the table for a fairly average screen size in absolute measurements. The other problem when the page resizes to fit the browser window is that the layout can change, so your designs might be messed up.

▶ Select the whole table by clicking the <table> tag at the bottom of the page.

▶ Click the Convert Table Widths to Pixels icon at the bottom of the Properties inspector. The width should be about 800 pixels.

▶ Now click the Convert Table Heights to Pixels icon. The height may have already been displayed in pixels in which case nothing will have changed. The height should be about 1000 pixels.

ⓘ You could change the table widths and heights back to % at any time by clicking the Convert Widths/Heights to Percent icons (next to the Convert Widths/Heights to Pixels icons).

Saving the template

It's important to save your work regularly. You save a template in just the same way as you would a normal page.

▶ Make sure the main_template page tab is selected at the bottom of the screen, just above properties. Select File, Save from the menu.

▶ You'll see a message about editable regions – we'll create these later. Click OK.

ⓘ When saving a template that you have based another page on you will get the following message. Don't worry – just click Yes and Dreamweaver will do all the hard work and update all the relevant pages for you. Click Close in the Update Pages dialogue box when it has finished updating.

Figure 3.13

Inserting Images

Now we'll start inserting images in the various sections of the table. For this we'll use the Insert Image icon on the Insert bar.

 Place the cursor in the second row. Click the Image icon on the Insert bar. ———

Figure 3.14: Locating the image file

 The image you want is in the Images folder. Click to select alperetreats_logo.jpg then click OK.

The image appears in the second row.

Figure 3.15: The image appears where the cursor was

Previewing the template

It's very easy to see what the template will look like when viewed in a browser.

 Before previewing any page or template you should save it first. If you don't save, the latest changes might not be shown in the browser. Select File, Save from the menu. Click OK to the message about editable regions.

 You might get a message about updating other documents based on the template – you don't have any pages based on this template yet so just click No.

 To preview the template in Internet Explorer, just press F12.

To preview the template in a different browser, select **File**, **Preview in Browser** from the main menu bar. If the browser you want isn't listed, select **Edit Browser List**....

Figure 3.16: Changing browser settings using the preferences window

 The **Preferences** window appears. To add a browser, just click the small + button at the top of the window. You'll then be asked to locate the browser software on your computer. You can also select a shortcut key for the new browser (**F12** is the default shortcut for **Internet Explorer**).

Figure 3.17: Previewing the template in Internet Explorer

This is exactly how you would view any page you create in **Dreamweaver**.

 You can leave the browser window open while you work on the page in Dreamweaver, but it won't update to reflect any changes you make in Dreamweaver. Each time you make a change, you will need to run through the steps above to preview the page.

Borders

Notice that the borders of the cells in the table are invisible. We'll just quickly run through the different options you could choose. You may not like the look of visible borders, but they can sometimes be useful.

 Return to the Dreamweaver window. Select the table using the <table> tag, and look at the table properties.

Figure 3.18: Table properties

The properties that affect the table borders are:

CellPad

Cell padding is the space around the contents of a cell.

CellSpace

Cell spacing is the space between cells in the table.

Border

You can enter a value for the border. Entering 0 gives an invisible border. The higher the number the thicker the border around the table. The default value is 1.

Brdr Color

You can choose a border colour. You can choose a border colour for the whole table, a row or a cell. Remember if you want a coloured border you'll have to change the Border value to 1; if it is 0 you won't see it!

BgColor

You can change the background colour in the table, a row or an individual cell.

Changing the background colour

We'll change the colour of one of the cells.

 Click in the last cell in row 3.

 In the Properties inspector at the bottom of the screen, click the small grey square labelled Bg.

Figure 3.19: The colour palette

▶ A dropper appears. You can select any colour on your screen with this – you aren't restricted to using one in the colour palette. Choose a colour of your own, or click the orange colour as shown above.

Figure 3.20

The cell is now coloured orange.

Assets and Favourites

In the **Files** panel group there is the **Assets** panel. The Assets panel contains every image, colour etc that you use in your web page. You can also make any asset a **Favourite**. We're going to add a colour to the **Favourites**.

Figure 3.21: The Assets panel

▶ Click the **Assets** panel in the **Files** panel group. Click the **Images** icon on the left of the panel. At the top of the panel make sure **Site** is selected and not **Favourites** as shown above.

▶ Take a look at what's there. It has listed all the *images* in the Images folder.

▶ In the **Assets** panel, click the **Colours** icon on the left. Notice that the colour you chose has not yet been added to the Assets panel. You need to refresh the panel first.

Refresh the panel by clicking the Refresh icon at the bottom of the panel.

Figure 3.22: The Assets panel lists the colours used

The orange colour has now appeared in the **Assets** panel. Now we're going to add the grey colour of the logo to the **Assets** panel. This grey is not in the colour palette so we'll use the dropper to click on the actual logo.

 Click in the first cell in row **3**. Now scroll up so that the Alpe Retreats logo is visible. Click the grey square labelled **Bg** in the **Properties** inspector.

Figure 3.23: Using the dropper to select a colour outside the colour palette

 Now click on the **Alpe Retreats** logo with the dropper as shown above.

 Refresh the **Assets** panel. The grey should appear alongside the orange.

Adding to Favourites

Adding any assets to Favourites is very straightforward. Adding an asset to **Favourites** is useful when you have so many assets that it is difficult to find any particular one. You would add an asset to **Favourites** if it was going to be used more than the others.

 Click on the grey colour in the **Assets** window. Click the **Add to Favourites** icon at the bottom of the panel.

▶ Click OK to the above message. Click the Favourites radio button at the top of the Assets panel. The grey colour should be there.

▶ Add the orange colour as well. These two colours will be used as the theme for the site, and will be used again.

▶ Save your template by selecting File, Save from the menu. Select OK at the prompt about editable regions.

Using Favourite colours

The way you use Favourites depends on the type of asset you are applying the colour to.

ⓘ For objects, select the object, select the colour in the Favourites panel and click the Apply button.

ⓘ For background colours it works slightly differently. You can't just select the cell then the colour and click apply. Instead, make sure the Favourites panel is showing the colour you want, select a cell in the table, then click Bg in the Properties inspector. Use the dropper to click on the colour in the Favourites panel. This is most useful when you want a custom colour (that you have previously added to Favourites), and nothing else on the page is the same colour, so the only thing you can click with the dropper is in the Favourites panel.

Finish off the colour scheme to look like the one below.

Figure 3.25

▶ Save the template then preview it by pressing the F12 key.

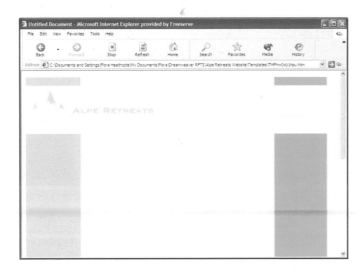

Figure 3.26

▶ Save your template by selecting File, Save from the menu.

Editable Regions

When you base a web page on a template, all content that is not specifically made an editable region is locked. As a result, in order to be able to add any content to the page, you need to specify editable regions on the template.

We will define two editable regions in the centre of the template so that content can be added in the white area below the logo.

▶ Click in the centre cell in row 3.

▶ In the Insert bar at the top of the screen, click the Templates tab. ———— Templates

Figure 3.27: The templates section of the Insert bar

▶ Click the Editable Region icon. You are now asked to enter a name for the editable region.

Figure 3.28: Naming an editable region

▶ Enter PageTitle in the Name box. Click OK.

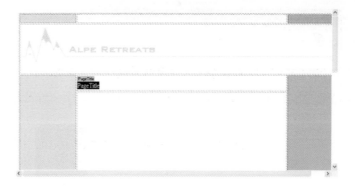

Figure 3.29

▶ Repeat this for the cell below, naming the editable region **PageContent**.

The second editable region will appear quite low down the page because it has been put in the middle of a very long cell. We'll re-align the editable regions to be at the top of each cell.

Aligning cell content

The editable regions appear in the centre of each cell because the properties of the cell specify that the contents should be aligned in the centre. It is not because of the properties of the editable regions.

▶ Click somewhere in the cell containing the first editable region, but click outside the editable region. Now click the <td> tag in the tag selector.

▶ In the Properties inspector, change the Vert property from Default to Top.

You will only notice a small change because the cell is so small.

▶ Repeat this for the second editable region. This time you should notice a big change of position, as the editable region moves to the top of the cell.

Figure 3.30

HTML Styles

First we'll create a new style then apply it to the PageTitle text.

▶ Click the New Style icon at the bottom of the Design panel.

The Define New Style window appears. Here you enter all the properties of the style.

▶ Enter the Font and Size properties as shown below.

Figure 3.31: Defining a new HTML Style

▶ Click the Bold icon.

▶ Change the colour of the text by clicking the small Color box below the Size property. Click the dropper on the grey background you've already got on the left of the page.

▶ Name the style you've just defined as PageTitle by entering it in the Name box at the top of the window.

Figure 3.32: Defining a new HTML Style

Click **OK**. The style now appears in the **HTML Styles** panel.

Figure 3.33: The HTML Styles panel

Now we'll apply that style to the text in the first editable region.

Double-click the text **PageTitle** in the first editable region so that it is selected (it is the text with the white background we want to select, not the blue background).

Click the **PageTitle** style in the **HTML Styles** panel.

The style of the text changes, and takes on the properties of the **PageTitle** style.

Figure 3.34

Now we'll do the same for the **PageContent** text.

Click the **New Style** icon in the **HTML Styles** panel. Enter the details as shown below.

Figure 3.35: Defining the PageContent style

Now apply the **PageContent** style to the text in the second editable region, just as you did the first.

Figure 3.36

Save the page either by selecting **File**, **Save** from the menu or by right-clicking on its page tab and selecting **Save** from the context menu.

Adding a Navigation bar

The best place to put a navigation bar is on the template – then it automatically appears on every page on your site (assuming every page uses the template).

We want the navigation bar to appear down the left of the page, in the grey area.

Click in the large grey cell on the left of the template.

On the **Insert** bar, click the **Common** tab. ——————————

Common

Now click the **Navigation Bar** icon. ——————————

Tip:
You can type in the colour code next to the **Color** box instead of using the dropper. The grey we used has the code **#999999**.

Figure 3.37: Inserting a Navigation Bar

Each nav bar **Element** is basically a button, or option. We're going to have 6 buttons (or elements).

For each element you need to specify a name, and which image is displayed when the button is up, down or when the mouse is over it. You will have downloaded all the necessary images in Chapter 2.

▶ The first button will be the **Home** button. Enter **Home** as the **Element Name**.

▶ Click the **Browse** button next to the **Up Image** box.

▶ The image you want is in **Images**, **nav_bar_buttons**.

Figure 3.38: Inserting a nav bar image

⊳ Locate the home_up.jpg image. Select it and then click OK.

⊳ For the Over Image, select home_over.jpg.

You don't need to enter any more images, Dreamweaver will automatically use the Up Image (home_up) for any of the conditions for which you haven't specified an image.

Since we haven't created the Home page yet, we won't enter a URL in the When Clicked, Go To URL field just yet – we can come back and do this later.

Adding an element

⊳ To add another button, just click the plus button at the top of the window. ────── **+**

⊳ Enter Resort as the name.

⊳ Enter the Up Image and Over Image as resort_up and resort_over.

Entering all the other elements

⊳ Enter the other 4 elements: Chalets, Prices, Booking and Contact. Use the images with the relevant names in the nav_bar_buttons folder.

Figure 3.39: Inserting a nav bar

▶ When you have entered all the elements, change the **Insert** option at the bottom of the screen to **Vertically**. Make sure the **Use Tables** option is checked. Click **OK**.

Figure 3.40

The navigation bar appears – but rather low down!

 If you didn't get the option to insert the nav bar vertically, or you forgot to select it: Insert a table **1** column X **6** rows where the nav bar should be. Click and drag each button from its current position into a row in the table. Resize the table cells so that the nav bar looks like the one above.

▶ Shift the nav bar up to the top of the cell by changing the properties of the cell. The easiest way to do this is to click on the nav bar then click the <td> tag to select the whole cell (the cell that contains the whole nav bar – not one of the cells that makes up the nav bar). Now adjust the **Vert** property of the cell in the **Properties** inspector to **Top**.

▶ Adjust the width of the cell to just cover the nav bar.

▶ Save the template.

Figure 3.41

Testing!

▶ Preview your template in a browser (press **F12** for Internet Explorer).

▶ Move the mouse over each of the buttons – the image should change to one with an orange dot inside the white one! If it doesn't, you'll get a chance to edit your nav bar in a minute.

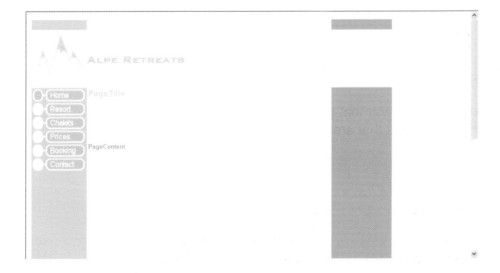

Figure 3.42

Editing the nav bar

If you want to change the order of the buttons, or the images, you'll need to edit your nav bar.

 Click the Nav Bar icon on the Insert bar – just as you did when you created it.

Figure 3.43

Click OK to the message that appears. Make any adjustments you need to, then click OK.

Saving and closing the template

Select File, Save from the main menu bar.

To close the template, *either*

Make sure the template page is selected (the page tab will be white, not grey) then select File, Close from the menu.

or

Right-click the template page tab and select Close from the shortcut menu.

Exiting Dreamweaver

Close Dreamweaver by first making sure all pages are closed, then selecting File, Exit from the menu.

You'll be pleased to hear that you've finished making the template! The next step is to create some pages that are based on this template.

Tip:
If you want to change the order of the buttons you can do this easily in the **Insert Navigation Bar** window. Just click on an element and use the small arrow icons above the **Nav Bar Elements** list to move the element up or down the list.

Tip:
You can also close Dreamweaver by clicking the red **Close** icon in the top right-hand corner of the window.

Chapter 4
Creating the Home Page

You've created the template that all the pages in your site will be based on. The first page we'll create will be the Home page.

▶ Load Dreamweaver (look back at the start of Chapter 2 if you need reminding how).

Dreamweaver automatically opens a new page called Untitled-1 when it is loaded. We'll close it now without saving.

▶ Right-click the Untitled-1 page tab. Select Close from the context menu.

Now we'll open a new page based on the template.

▶ Select File, New from the menu.

▶ Click the Templates tab; the text will change to New From Template in the top of the window.

▶ Choose the same settings as shown below.

Figure 4.1: Opening a new page based on a template

▶ Click **Create**.

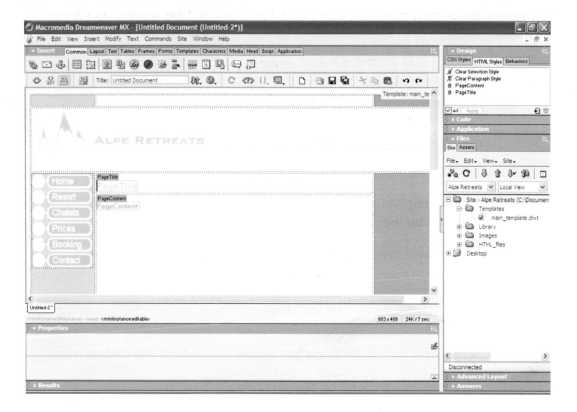

Figure 4.2

▶ Try changing any part of the template that you didn't specify as **Editable** – it will be locked.

Adding text

We're going to insert the page title in the first editable region.

▶ Click where it says **Page Title** (with the white background, not blue). Delete the text **PageTitle** and type **Home**.

Figure 4.3

Inserting a table

Now we'll insert a table into the second editable region to help arrange the page better.

▶ Delete the text PageContent. Leave the cursor in the editable region.

▶ Click the Insert Table icon in the Insert bar. ──────────

▶ Enter the settings as shown below. Click OK.

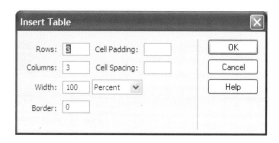

Figure 4.4: Inserting a table

Saving the Home page

▶ Right-click the page tab (called something like Untitled-2) and select Save from the menu.

Figure 4.5: Inserting a table

ℹ Whilst most of your html files should be saved in the HTML_files folder, many servers like the home page file to be in the root directory – that is in the Alpe Retreats Website folder.

▶ Locate the Alpe Retreats Website folder, name the file index.html and click Save. It is extremely important that you save the file with that name because nearly all servers will look for a file called index.html to display when a user logs on to the site. If you don't have a file named index.html (or index.htm) you'll just get a blank page instead of the Home page.

Tip:
Don't forget to include the **.html** file extension. If you leave this off Dreamweaver will add the extension **.htm**. This isn't a big problem, but it is safer to use **.html**. If you have saved the file as a **.htm** file, right-click the file in the **Site** panel and select **Rename** from the context menu.

Inserting an Image

 Click the cursor in the last cell in row 2 of the new table. Click the Insert Image icon on the Insert bar.

Figure 4.6: Inserting an image

 Locate the chalet_vert.jpg file under Images, chalet_photos. Select it and then click OK.

The image probably hasn't been put exactly where you want it. Adjust the table borders to look like the screenshot below.

Figure 4.7: Inserting an image

You can make the image appear in the middle of the cell by placing the cursor in the cell then clicking the <td> tag in the tag selector. Change the Horiz and Vert options in the Properties inspector.

Figure 4.8

Now add some text next to the picture. Either make up your own or copy the following screenshot.

 To add text, just click the cursor where you want the text to appear, then start typing! If the cursor appears in the wrong place, you may have to change the Horiz and Vert settings in the Properties inspector. We'll format the text to look better later on.

Figure 4.9: Entering text

Applying an HTML Style

We need to apply the PageContent style to the text you've just written.

Select the cell containing the text using the <td> tag. Now click PageContent in the HTML Styles panel. All the text in the cell should change to the PageContent style.

Don't forget to save your page regularly.

E-mail links

Look at the last sentence in Figure 4.9, we're going to make the word e-mail a hyperlink that opens a new e-mail to a specified e-mail address.

▶ Select the text e-mail.

 ▶ Click the Email Link icon on the Insert bar.

Figure 4.10: Inserting an e-mail link

▶ Enter the information as in Figure 4.10, or alternatively enter your own e-mail address. Click OK.

The text should now be blue and underlined – this is the standard way of displaying a hyperlink.

▶ Save and preview your home page.

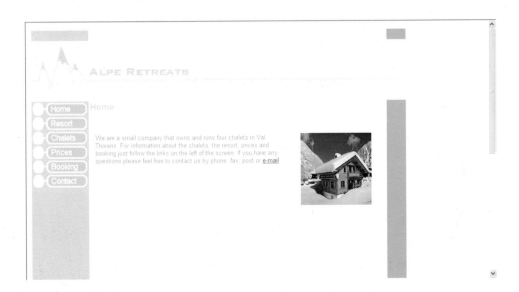

Figure 4.11

Notice that the orange stripe down the right of the page is being squashed. This is actually because the table in the second editable region has a width of 100%; when you preview the page in the browser it is trying to resize to be the width of the browser window. If we change the width to be in pixels it won't do this.

▶ In Dreamweaver, select the table in the second editable region using the <table> tag.

▶ Click the Convert Table Widths to Pixels icon in the Properties inspector.

▶ Save and preview the page again. This time the orange stripe should be the same width as it is in Dreamweaver.

Test it!

▶ Click the text e-mail. A new window appears where you can write and send an e-mail to the address you entered above.

Figure 4.12: Testing the e-mail link

▶ Try sending the e-mail if you like. Otherwise close the window by clicking the red Close icon. Keep the browser window open.

Tip:
An e-mail client must be set up for this to work. To do this, open **Internet Explorer** then select **Tools, Internet Options** from the menu. Under the **Programs** tab, make sure there is a program selected for e-mail, such as **Outlook Express**.

Adding a Page Title

Notice that in the top of the browser window it says Untitled Document. If you enter a Page Title it will appear here. This not only looks good, but is also quite important if you want your page to be picked up by search engines, as they will list search results under the Page Title of the page.

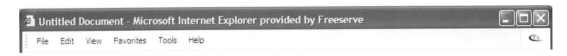

Figure 4.13: No page title

▶ Return to Dreamweaver. Notice that in the Document toolbar there is a field named Title that is currently saying Untitled Document.
(If you cannot see the Document toolbar, select View, Toolbars, Document from the main menu bar).

Figure 4.14: Entering a page title in Dreamweaver

▶ Change the Title to Alpe Retreats - Home. Now save the page and preview it again to see the effect.

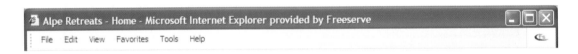

Figure 4.15

Tip:
When using a Search Engine, have you ever seen entries listed under a title starting with **Untitled?**
This is because whoever created that page did not add a page title!

Tip:
You will need to press **F12** again – your changes will not be reflected in any browser window that is already open.

Design and Code View

If you really want to see the HTML code that is behind your web page you must be in the correct view.

On the Document toolbar at the top of the screen there are three different View icons:

Figure 4.16: Different views

So far you have been working in Design View. This gives you the most accurate picture of how your web page will look in a Browser.

Code View shows you just the HTML code. This code will have been created by Dreamweaver, but you can edit the code directly here if you know what you're doing!

Code and Design View splits the window in two. In the top half is the Code View and in the bottom half the Design View. You can change the size of the two windows by clicking and dragging the border between the top and bottom window.

Figure 4.17: Code and Design View

Save and close the Home page

▶ Save the Home page by right-clicking the page tab and selecting Save from the context menu. If the option to Save is greyed-out, this is because the page is already saved.

▶ Close the page by selecting Close from the same context menu. Close any browser windows that are open.

▶ Close Dreamweaver if this is the end of a session.

Tip:
You can close a page by right-clicking on its page tab and selecting **Close** from the context menu.

Chapter 5
Creating the Resort Page

▶ First make sure that Dreamweaver is open.

▶ Select **File**, **New** from the menu.

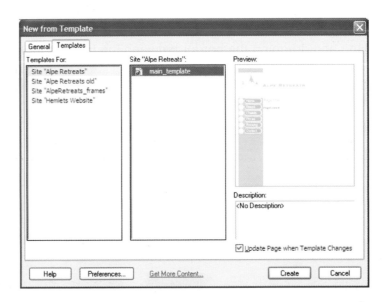

Figure 5.1: Opening a new page based on a template

▶ Set the options as they are in the screenshot above then click **Create**.

▶ Replace the text **PageTitle** with the text **Resort Information**.

Now you need to build the bulk of the page. The main steps you need to go through are listed below; if you can't remember how to do something, just look back over the last few chapters – you've already covered everything you need.

▶ Enter a **Title** for the **Resort** page.

▶ Create the table (**5** rows x **3** columns) in the second editable region, and edit it so that it is the right shape by dragging the table borders. It will look better if the table is invisible so enter a **Border** value of **0**. Remember that if you leave the width as **100%** the table can obscure the orange stripe on the right of the page; convert the table widths to pixels. Don't worry about the heights of the cells, these will resize to fit the text you will type in.

▶ Then enter the text – you can either copy the screenshot or just make up your own. Make sure all the text is in the right style.

▶ Now insert the images to go with each paragraph of text. The file names of the images you need are labelled in the screenshot below, and are in the Images folder.

Figure 5.2

Tip:
You can resize images by first selecting them so that small black handles appear. Hold down the **Shift** key then click and drag one of the corner handles. Release the mouse when you're happy with the size.

▶ We want the text to be spread out so that not all of it fits on the screen at any one time. Select the whole table using the <table> tag then click and drag the bottom handle to make it about as long as the template.

▶ Save the page as Resort by selecting File, Save from the menu.

▶ Preview your site in a browser to see how it looks.

Figure 5.3: Previewing the Resort page

Looking good! Don't worry that there is a lot of wasted space on the page – this is deliberate because we need the text to be long in order to show exactly what Named Anchors are useful for – we'll do this now.

Named Anchors

There is quite a lot of text on this page, and if previewed in a small browser window people would have to scroll down to the information they are interested in. Named Anchors allow you to click on a menu item at the top of a page and be taken to a specific place on the same page.

▶ In Dreamweaver, place the cursor at the end of the text in the top editable region and press Return to get a new line.

▶ Enter the text as shown below. Use the PageContent HTML Style.

Figure 5.4

Now we'll insert the anchors.

▶ Place the cursor to the left of the first word in the first paragraph (i.e. to the left of Val Thorens)

▶ Click the Named Anchor icon on the Insert bar.

Figure 5.5: Creating a Named Anchor

When asked to name it, enter Resort. Click OK.

A small anchor symbol will appear where the cursor was. This won't appear in a browser – it will be invisible.

Figure 5.6: The anchor is shown in Dreamweaver, but will be invisible in a browser

Repeat this for the 3 other paragraphs, naming the anchors ApresSki, Weather and Maps.

Now we need to set up hyperlinks to link the words at the top with each anchor.

Double-click on the word Resort in the first editable region. Look at the Properties inspector at the bottom of the screen; there is a property called Link that should currently be blank.

Figure 5.7: The Link property is used to create hyperlinks

Click and drag the target symbol next to the Link field onto the first named anchor, so that it says #Resort in the Link field, then drop.

Repeat this for the other 3 items, ApresSki, Weather and Maps.

Finally, create a named anchor at the top of the screen and then link the Back to Top text (at the bottom of the page) to it.

Test it! Save the page and preview it in a browser. Click on all the links you've just created.

Hyperlinks to other web sites

Notice that in the Weather section there is a reference to the Val Thorens official web site. We are going to make a hyperlink that will open the Val Thorens web site in a new browser window.

Select the text www.valthorens.com. We need to enter the web site address in the Link field in the Properties inspector.

Type in the text http://www.valthorens.com in the **Link** field in the **Properties** inspector.

Figure 5.8: The Link property

Opening the site in another window

At the moment the hyperlink is opening the new site in the same window – effectively closing your site!

 Select the **Val Thorens** hyperlink on the page. In the **Properties** inspector select **_blank** from the menu in the **Target** field. Selecting **_blank** always means that the link will open in a new (blank) window.

Figure 5.9: Opening a link in a new window

 Save the page then preview it to see that the links work properly. You'll need to be online to check the external links.

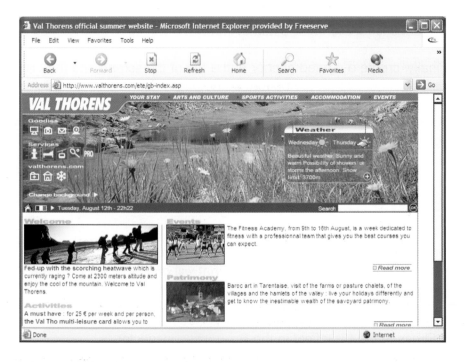

Figure 5.10: The Val Thorens web site in August

The Maps link

Notice that it says in the maps info to click here to go straight to the maps part of the Val Thorens site. This link should actually link to a specific page within the Val Thorens web site. You can do this by logging on to the Val Thorens web site (www.valthorens.com), going to the Maps page then copying the address in the Address bar. You can they paste this address into the Link field in the Properties inspector.

 The web site address is http://www.valthorens.com/ete/gb-plans.asp?plan=station – quite a mouthful! This is why it's often easier to use copy and paste rather than trying to type it.

 Test the link. Save and close the Resort page.

Accessibility

There are things you can add to your web site to make it much easier to view for someone who is blind or partially-sighted. There is software available that will read text on a screen, and any other text you might have hidden on the page for this purpose. For example, you can attach text to an image that can be read out to someone browsing your site. In fact, you can attach text to a variety of objects in Dreamweaver.

 Select Edit, Preferences from the menu bar.

Figure 5.11: Accessibility options in the Preferences window

 Check the boxes next to the objects that you want to add alternative text to. Just select Images to begin with. Click OK.

 Open up the index.html page. Delete the chalet photo and re-insert it.

Figure 5.12: Adding accessibility features to an image

The Image Tag Accessibility Attributes window appears. Type something suitable in the Alternative Text and Long Description fields. Click OK.

How accessible is your site?

Dreamweaver can generate a report listing all the parts of the page that aren't deemed accessible.

Click away from the photo you've just inserted. Select File, Check Page, Check Accessibility from the menu.

The Results panel group appears containing an accessibility report.

Click and drag the border between the Properties panel and the blank workspace to make the Results panel group bigger.

Tip:
The red cross means that the item is not accessible. The question mark means that the item might cause some confusion.

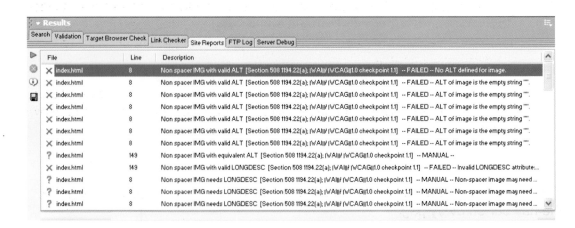

Figure 5.13: An Accessibility report

There are quite a few items here! This is because none of the images in the template have alternative text. Try adding some more alternative text to the images on the template and running the report again.

Tip:
Close the Results panel group by clicking the icon at the top right of the group and selecting Close Panel Group from the menu

Chapter 6
Layers

In this chapter you'll be creating the Chalets page. Like the other pages, the bulk of the Chalets page is made up of images and text set in a table which you are already familiar with. The difference with this page is that it is actually four pages, not one (one page for each chalet). We will create a second menu that appears when the Chalets nav bar button is pressed, from which you can select the chalet you wish to see.

This will give you a useful introduction to both Layers and Behaviours, both of which might sound a bit advanced, but this really is quite straightforward, and the extra menu will add a really professional touch to your site. The Behaviours will be covered in the next chapter.

Layers

Layers are useful for two main reasons:

 They are good for layout because they allow you to overlap items and place one thing on top of another (which is not possible without layers). If an object is placed in its own layer, you can place it anywhere on the page, without using a table.

 You can attach Behaviours to layers. The Behaviours we will be using are Show and Hide. The menu layer will be hidden most of the time, and shown when the mouse is over the Chalets nav bar button.

Creating a new layer

The new layer will be part of the template because we want it to appear alongside the nav bar on every page.

 Open the main_template.dwt file by double-clicking it in the Site panel.

Figure 6.1: The Layers panel

The layers are listed in the Layers panel which is in the Advanced Layout panel group. As you can see there are no layers currently created.

Insert a new layer by clicking the Draw Layer icon in the Insert bar.

 Drag out a small rectangle as shown below.

Figure 6.2: Drawing a layer

Now we'll insert a table into the new layer.

Use the Insert Table icon on the Insert bar to insert a table 4 rows x 1 column. The cursor must be in the new layer in order that the table is inserted in the layer.

Figure 6.3: Inserting a table into a layer

 Type the following text into the table:

Figure 6.4

Resizing the layer

The text in your layer might run onto 2 lines, in which case you need to widen it.

▶ If the handles are not visible, move the cursor over the edge of the layer so that it becomes a cross-headed arrow, as shown below, and click.

Figure 6.5: Selecting a layer

▶ You should now see small black handles around the layer. You can click and drag these handles to resize the layer.

Figure 6.6: Resizing a layer

Changing the table background colour

▶ We want to colour the background orange, but leave a white space between the cells. To do this, leave the table background settings as they are, and change the cell backgrounds individually. Just click in a cell, and change the **Bg** property to orange (click the dropper on the nav bar to perfectly match the colours).

Figure 6.7: Changing the cell background colours

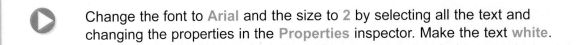 Change the font to Arial and the size to 2 by selecting all the text and changing the properties in the Properties inspector. Make the text white.

Naming the layer

It is always a good idea to name layers so that you can easily recognise which layer is which when they are listed in the Advanced Layout panel.

Figure 6.8: Selecting the cell to display layer properties

Select the layer by clicking on the top left layer handle (shown above) to display the layer properties in the Properties inspector.

Figure 6.9: Layer properties

Enter SubMenu as the LayerID.

If you look in the Advanced Layout panel the layer should now be listed under its new name.

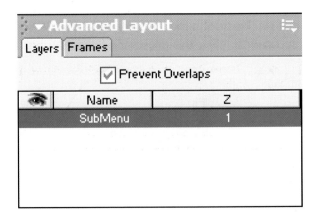

Figure 6.10: The SubMenu layer is displayed in the Layers panel

Hiding the layer

You can show and hide a layer whilst designing a site using the Advanced Layout panel.

 In the column that has an eye in the header, click next to the layer. A closed-eye symbol will appear and the layer will disappear.

Figure 6.11: Showing and hiding a layer

 Keep clicking in the same place; the layer will cycle through three phases: hidden, visible and unspecified. Leave the layer hidden, with the closed-eye icon.

Save!

 Don't forget to save your work regularly. When you save you will get the following message because you have two pages based on the template. Just click Yes and then Close when the pages are updated.

Figure 6.12: Saving a template

Creating the chalet pages

You need to create 4 new pages, each of which will be named after a chalet and will contain an image and some text about that chalet. We will then set up hyperlinks to link the menu items with each of the pages.

▶ Open 4 new pages based on the main_template, saving them as ChaletVert, ChaletBlanche, ChaletRouge and ChaletNoir.

▶ In the Images folder there are images for each of the chalets, named after the chalets. Insert the images and some text so that the pages look something like the one below.

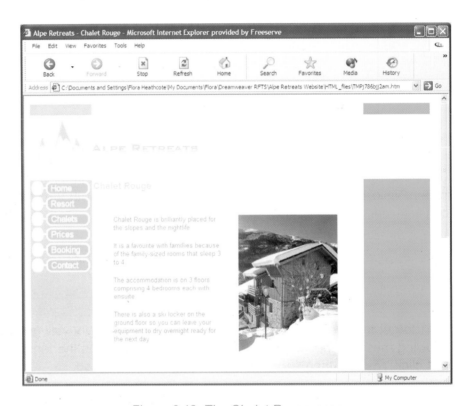

Figure 6.13: The Chalet Rouge page

Save all

When you are creating and editing a lot of pages at once you can save all instead of individually saving pages.

▶ Select File, Save All from the menu.

▶ Close the four chalet pages you have just created.

Creating the hyperlinks

▶ Return to the template and unhide the SubMenu layer.

▶ Highlight the text Chalet Vert in the SubMenu layer.

Tip:
When you insert the chalet photos you will probably get a prompt about **Alternative Text** – this is because you have the Image accessibility checked in **Preferences**. (see page 57 to uncheck this option.)

Tip:
To speed things up, you could copy the table, text and image from the first chalet page you create and paste it into the others, changing only some of the text and the image. To do this, select the table using the **<table>** tag just above the properties panel and select **Edit, Copy** from the menu. Go to the second chalet page, place the cursor in the editable region and select **Edit, Paste** from the menu.

Make sure all the html files of the chalet pages are visible in the Site panel.

Figure 6.14: The Site panel

Tip:
If you don't like using the target, click the **Browse** icon to the right of the target. Now find and select the file you want and then click **OK**.

 In the Properties inspector, click and drag the target next to the Link field onto the ChaletVert.htm file and drop.

The text should now be underlined to signify a hyperlink.

 Repeat this for the other menu items, linking them to the relevant chalet pages.

Figure 6.15: Creating hyperlinks

 Save your template. Close the template if this is the end of a session, otherwise leave it open for the next chapter.

Chapter 7
Behaviours

In this chapter we'll add the behaviours that will make the SubMenu layer appear when the mouse is on the Chalets nav bar button. The submenu will disappear again when either a submenu option is selected or the mouse is no longer over the Chalets button or the SubMenu layer.

▶ Open the template if it is not already open.

▶ Click the Chalets button on the nav bar. Make sure you can see the Behaviours panel in the Design panel group. See that there are already some Behaviours here that Dreamweaver created for you when you designed the nav bar.

Tip:
If you can't see the **Behaviours** panel, select **Window, Behaviours** from the menu.

Figure 7.1: The Behaviours panel

Choosing a browser version

Some behaviours don't work in earlier browsers, so you can select which behaviours are available to you according to which browsers you want them to work in.

▶ Click the plus symbol near the top of the Behaviours panel.

▶ Select Show Events For from the menu. You can now choose a browser. If you have it, select IE 4.0.

Figure 7.2: Choosing a browser version

Adding a new behaviour

▶ To add a new behaviour, just click the plus button at the top of the behaviours window.

Figure 7.3: Selecting the type of behaviour

▶ Select Show-Hide Layers from the menu.

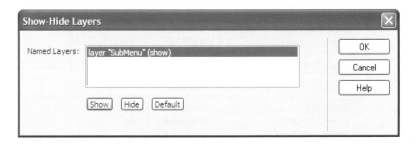

Figure 7.4: The Show-Hide Layers behaviour

▶ Click the Show button at the bottom of the Show-Hide Layers window; (show) should appear beside the layer name. Click OK.

At the moment, the Show-Hide Layers action is dependent on the onClick event (this is the default option). We need to change it to onMouseOver.

▶ In the Design panel, click the small down-arrow next to the text OnClick in the Events column. Now select onMouseOver from the menu that appears.

The **Behaviours** panel should now look like this:

Figure 7.6: The Behaviours panel

Now create another behaviour. The **Action** will be to **Hide** the **SubMenu** layer, and the **Event** will be **onMouseOut**. The method is the same as that used above, so refer to that if you get stuck. Make sure the **Chalets** nav bar button is still selected or you'll attach the behaviour to something else!

Figure 7.7: The Behaviours panel

Hide the layer using the **Advanced Layout** panel. Save the template.

Now preview the template in a browser. The submenu should appear and disappear as you move the mouse over the **Chalets** button.

Adding behaviours to the layer

We will attach another couple of behaviours to the layer itself. We want to show the layer when the mouse is over the layer, and hide it if the mouse leaves the layer. What we then need to do is move the layer close enough to the Chalets button so that the mouse can be over the layer before leaving the Chalets button. If we don't do this, the layer will disappear before the mouse gets to it!

▶ Show the layer using the Advanced Layout panel so that you can work on it.

▶ Select the layer – make sure you've selected the whole layer, if so Layer ID should be displayed in the Properties inspector.

▶ Click the plus button in the Behaviours panel to add a new behaviour. ——— ⊞

▶ Select Show-Hide Layers from the menu then click the Show button in the Show-Hide Layers window. Click OK.

▶ Change the Event from onClick to onMouseOver.

▶ Create a second behaviour to Hide the layer onMouseOut.

Figure 7.8: The Behaviours panel

Moving the layer

You need to move the layer so that it is just touching the Chalets button. This will take some trial and error, as the layer often appears in a slightly different place to where you think when you preview it in a browser!

 Click and drag the layer so that it is touching the Chalets button. Preview the page in a browser.

Figure 7.9: The SubMenu layer in Design view

Figure 7.10: The SubMenu layer in Preview mode

The two screenshots above show the layer in what's supposed to be the same position, in Design and in Preview mode.

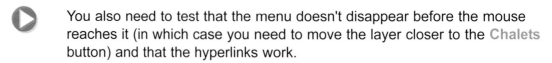 You also need to test that the menu doesn't disappear before the mouse reaches it (in which case you need to move the layer closer to the Chalets button) and that the hyperlinks work.

When you are happy with the position of the layer, set it to hidden in the Advanced Layout panel so that when you preview the page it will be hidden until the mouse moves over the Chalets button.

Save your template.

Setting up the hyperlinks for the nav bar

Since you are already editing the template, now would be a good time to enter the hyperlinks for the nav bar, for the Home and Resort pages.

▶ Click the Nav Bar icon on the Insert bar to edit the existing nav bar. ⎯⎯⎯⎯⎯⎯

▶ In the Modify Navigation Bar window, click the Browse button next to the When Clicked, Go To URL: field.

▶ Find the index.html file and click OK.

▶ Repeat this for the Resort button.

Figure 7.11: Adding hyperlinks to the nav bar

▶ Click OK.

Save

▶ Save the template and then preview it. Test that the buttons take you to the correct pages.

▶ Close the template, and Dreamweaver too if this is the end of a session.

Tip:
If you don't save the template before previewing it, the changes may not be reflected in the browser. It is always best to save a page first before previewing it.

Chapter 8
Tables of Data

In this chapter you'll be creating the Prices page. This is essentially a large table of data, and you have already learned most of the features you need to do this.

▶ Open Dreamweaver if it is not already open.

▶ Create a new page based on the template and save it in the HTML_files folder as Prices.html.

▶ Add the page title, Prices and Availability. Also add the title Alpe Retreats – Prices and Availability in the Title field of the Document toolbar at the top of the screen.

Figure 8.1: Adding the page title on the page and the toolbar

Because the prices table is quite big, quite a large table is needed. We'll create the prices table inside another table to make its positioning easier.

 ▶ Create the first table, 3 columns x 3 rows. Resize it so that it covers most of the page, with the centre cell much larger than the rest (see Figure 8.2).

Figure 8.2

The prices table will go in the centre cell of the first table; the first table is there to help you position the prices table exactly where you want it on the page.

▶ Place the cursor in the centre cell, then click the Insert Table icon to insert the second table.

Figure 8.3: Inserting a table

▶ Enter the table rows and columns as shown above. Click OK.

▶ Merge some of the cells in the top row of this table using the Merge Cells icon in the Properties inspector, so that your table looks like Figure 8.4.

Figure 8.4: Merging cells

Enter the column headings, row headings and data as shown in the table below (it doesn't matter if you make up your own, or even if you leave some cells empty).

Date	Chalet Vert		Chalet Blanche		Chalet Rouge		Chale Noir	
	£Price	Avail	£Price	Avail	£Price	Avail	£Price	Avail
13th Dec	425	12	445	16	489	11	519	4
20th Dec	569	4	599	4	665	8	765	FULL
27th Dec	765	FULL	775	FULL	839	11	919	FULL
3rd Jan	505	8	545	10	509	4	535	4
10th Jan	525	12	549	10	555	5	539	6
17th Jan	549	12	549	6	585	6	639	8
24th Jan	575	10	579	10	615	7	645	FULL
31st Jan	579	4	625	8	635	11	669	FULL
7th Feb	585	6	639	16	679	FULL	695	FULL
14th Feb	789	2	765	FULL	809	4	909	4
21st Feb	735	4	715	FULL	759	8	859	FULL
28th Feb	635	8	615	2	679	FULL	745	FULL
6th Mar	575	6	599	FULL	669	11	729	2
13th Mar	565	4	549	4	655	FULL	719	6
20th Mar	539	8	539	8	645	4	715	FULL
27th Mar	535	6	535	4	629	2	695	6
3rd Apr	549	10	565	6	605	7	675	2
10th Apr	625	8	555	10	649	7	685	4
17th Apr	539	12	505	16	599	4	635	FULL

Figure 8.5: Entering text and data

Notice that the current availability is shown on this page. The availability figure will need to be updated regularly by someone at Alpe Retreats. You will learn how to update a web page later when you learn how to get your web page online.

Resizing table columns

You may need to resize the columns to fit the data on one line – the table will become twice as long if each line of data runs onto two lines.

▶ Click and drag the table borders to resize the columns. This can be rather frustrating; a little time and patience should do the trick though.

▶ Finally add some text below the table as shown below.

Figure 8.6

▶ Save the page then preview it in a browser to see what it looks like.

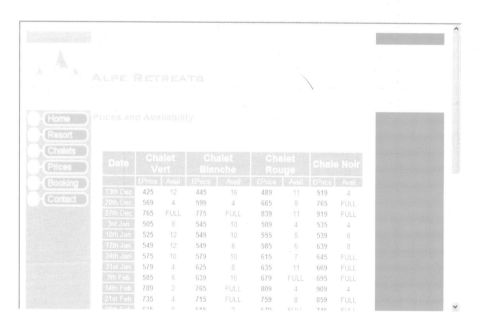

Figure 8.7: Previewing the page

That's the Prices page finished!

▶ Save and close the page.

▶ Open the main_template.dwt file and add the hyperlink for the Prices button on the nav bar. Save and preview the site and flick between all the pages you've done so far to check they work as expected.

Tip:
If the orange border on the right is narrower when you preview the page, this is because you haven't converted the table widths to pixels. Do this then check again that the border looks OK.

Chapter 9
Forms

In this chapter you'll create the Booking page. This will involve using Forms, which we haven't covered yet. The form will be filled in by the customer online, and then sent to the host of the Alpe Retreats site by e-mail.

The information from a form is collected in something called a script. The script can be written in a variety of programming languages, and can be sent to a specified location (including an e-mail address). There are many options here, and there may be specific reasons why you may want to use one programming language over another – one of which is the facilities provided by your ISP (Internet Service Provider). Here it will be assumed that you have an ISP that supports a script being sent to a specified e-mail address. Don't worry if you don't have an ISP – we'll cover that in the next chapter.

The form container

All the fields in a form need to be held in a form container. This is just a simple box that will expand as you put more in it.

▶ Create a new page based on the template. Save the page as Booking.html.

Figure 9.1: Saving a page

▶ Change the Page Title to Booking.

▶ Delete the text PageContent in the second editable region.

▶ On the Insert bar, click the Forms tab.

Figure 9.2: The Forms section of the Insert bar

► Click the cursor in the PageContent editable region. Press Enter a couple of times to expand the editable region.

► Click the Form icon in the Insert bar. ————————————————

Figure 9.3: The form container is shown by a red dotted line

A red dotted line appears representing the form container. The cursor should now be inside the new form container, and the form properties should be displayed in the Properties inspector.

The best way to arrange the various elements of a form is usually to put them into a table. We'll create the table first then insert the elements in it.

Tip:
If you can't see the red dotted line you might have **Invisible Elements** switched off. To turn them on, select **View**, **Visual Aids**, **Invisible Elements** from the menu bar. It will have a small tick next to it if it's already selected.

Create the table

▷ Make sure the cursor is within the form container (**<Form>** will be highlighted at the bottom of the page, and the form properties will be displayed in the **Properties** inspector). Create a table with **15** rows and **7** columns.

Figure 9.4: Inserting a table

▷ Arrange the columns to look like the screenshot below.

Figure 9.5

▷ Merge the cells in the top row and add the following text:

Figure 9.6

Adding a text field

▶ In the second row, enter the label for the first text field, First Name. Give it the text style PageContent.

▶ Click the cursor in the next column (column 3) and click the Text Field icon ———— [▯] under the Forms tab on the Insert bar.

Figure 9.7: Inserting a text field

Tip:
Highlight the whole table and give it the style **PageContent**. That way, anything you type in any cell will have that style.

Naming fields

You should name all elements on the form. The form script will basically contain a list of field names and the values entered into these fields by the user. If you haven't named the fields this list of information will mean nothing, and will be much more difficult to process.

▶ Make sure the text field you just created is selected (click it if the field properties aren't showing in the Properties inspector).

▶ Enter FirstName (no spaces) into the field name box.

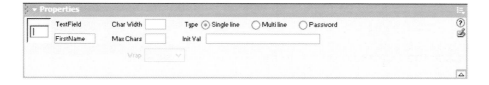

Figure 9.8: Naming a field

Changing the size of a text field

The text field is slightly longer than we want it. You cannot click and drag the borders of the field to resize it; instead you use the Properties inspector.

▶ In the Properties inspector, enter the Char Width property as 20. Press Enter.

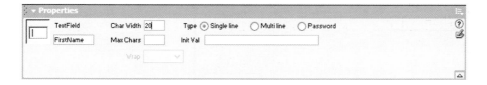

Figure 9.9: Changing the width of a field

Creating a List field

A List field is one where instead of typing in a value, you select it from a list. These fields are useful where there are only a limited number of values that field can take such as a Title field.

▶ In the fourth column, type Title.

▶ Click in the next column then click the List/Menu icon on the Insert bar (make sure the Forms tab is selected).

Figure 9.10: Inserting a List field

Take a look at the List field properties:

Figure 9.11: List field properties

▶ Name the field Title.

These fields can be used as menus as well as lists, but for now we want it to be a simple list.

▶ Click the List radio button in the Properties inspector.

Adding list values

Now you need to enter the values that will appear in the list.

▶ Click the List Values button in the Properties inspector.

▶ Enter Miss as the Item Label. Don't worry about entering a value.

Figure 9.12: Entering item labels

▶ Click the **+** button to add another value. Type **Mrs**.

▶ Add some more options so that your list looks like the one below.

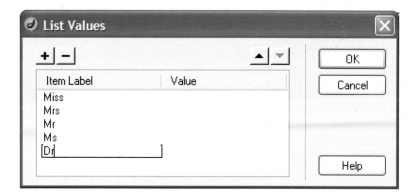

Figure 9.13: Entering item labels

▶ Click **OK** when you are happy with the list.

▶ In the **Properties** inspector, select **Mr** as the **Initially Selected** value.

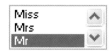

Figure 9.14: Selecting the Initially Selected value

Entering the other text and list fields

There are quite a few text fields and one list field that you now know how to create.

▶ Enter the labels and create the text fields shown in the screenshot below. Make sure you give each field a meaningful name and a **Char Width** of **20**.

Figure 9.15

▶ Create a **List** field for the **Chalet field**. Enter the four chalet names as the list values (**Chalet Vert**, **Chalet Blanche**, **Chalet Rouge**, **Chalet Noir**). Give the field a meaningful name. The width of the field will adjust automatically to the length of the list values you enter.

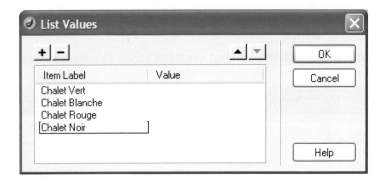

Figure 9.16: Entering List labels

▶ Don't forget to save your page regularly.

Radio buttons

Radio buttons are grouped, and the user can only select one button from the group. We will use radio buttons to ask the user how they would prefer Alpe Retreats to contact them.

▶ Add the fields **Week Commencing** and **Number in Group** as shown below.

▶ Enter the text from the screenshot below.

Figure 9.17

 ▶ Click the cursor in the next column then click the **Radio Group** icon on the **Insert** bar.

▶ Enter the information as it is in Figure 9.18. To enter values for the buttons, click on the word **Radio** in the list then type the text.

Figure 9.18: Radio Groups

Click **OK**. Your form should now look like the one below.

Figure 9.19: Radio Groups

 Save and preview your form.

Text Areas

Now we'll add a text area. This is a larger field where people can type any comments or questions they may have.

 Enter the text shown below, beginning **Please leave any comments....**

Figure 9.20

 Merge the next **4** columns in this row. Leave the cursor in the merged cell.

 Click the **Textarea** icon on the **Insert** bar.

 Adjust the **Char Width** and **Num Lines** properties so that the text area fills the cell.

Adding buttons

Finally, you need to add a couple of buttons. One of the buttons will **Clear** the form, and the other will **Submit** it.

 Place the cursor in one of the cells in the bottom right of the form. Click the **Button** icon on the **Insert** bar.

The button becomes a **Submit** button by default. Change the **Label** in the **Properties** inspector to **Submit Form**.

Figure 9.21: Submit button properties

 Add another button in the next column. Change the properties to look like this:

Figure 9.22: Reset button properties

Your form should look something like the one below:

The **Submit** button doesn't do anything at the moment; we'll cover that in the next chapter.

Figure 9.23

 Save and preview your form.

Another way of adjusting column widths

You have probably already noticed that adjusting column widths in large tables by clicking and dragging table borders can be quite frustrating because Dreamweaver just doesn't seem to do what it's asked. The other way to do this is just to enter column widths in the **Properties** inspector.

 Click in a cell in the column you want to adjust, then enter a value in the **W** field in the **Properties** inspector. This will adjust the width of the whole column, not just that cell. In the screenshot above, a width of **120 pixels** was used for each of the **4** main columns, and **10 pixels** for the **3** small columns. Change the table widths to pixels if they are currently in percent.

ℹ This method doesn't seem to work so well if there are a lot of merged cells in a table, such as the table on the Prices page.

Submitting the form

At the moment, clicking the Submit button will do nothing. To get this working, we will need to add code that will send the script (containing all the information entered by the user) to a specified e-mail address. This is actually much easier than it sounds – all you have to do is add a couple of entries in the Properties inspector.

▶ Click in one of the cells in the form.

▶ Select the whole form by clicking the <form> tag in the Tag selector. The whole form should be shaded grey to show that it is selected.

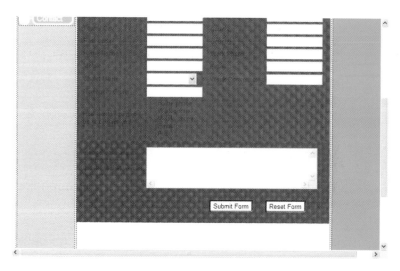

Figure 9.24: Selecting the whole form

▶ In the Properties inspector, name the form BookingForm by entering this in the FormName box.

▶ In the Action field, enter mailto:youremail@home.com, substituting your e-mail address where it says youremail@home.com. You must enter a valid e-mail address or you won't be able to test it properly.

▶ Enter the other details as shown in the screenshot below.

Figure 9.25: Form properties

▶ Save the Booking page then preview it in a browser.

▶ You can test the form even though your site isn't on a server yet. If you are online, preview the form and click the Submit button.

Figure 9.26: Your browser may generate this message about sending e-mails

▶ Click **Yes** to the prompt about whether or not you want to send an e-mail.

Figure 9.27: Outlook Express may generate this message about sending e-mails

▶ Click **Send**. You may get slightly different messages depending on which browser and e-mail client you are using.

▶ Check your inbox to see if it worked! If it doesn't work, go back to the **Booking** form in Dreamweaver and check the settings in the **Property** inspector.

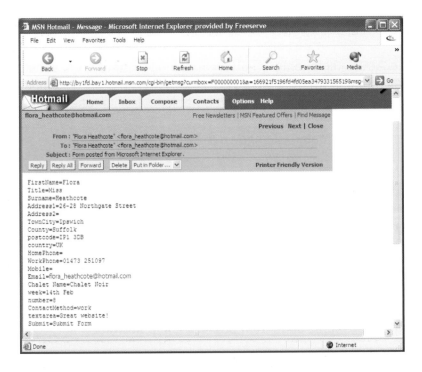

Figure 9.28: This is the e-mail that was sent from the Booking form

Tip:
This won't work if you're not online. Also, you need to make sure you have an e-mail client set up. If you're not sure, go to **Internet Explorer**, then select **Tools**, **Internet Options**. Click the **Programs** tab and make sure there is a program selected for e-mail. If not, choose something like **Outlook Express** if you have it.

Tip:
If you cannot get this to work, it's possible that it is because of the e-mail settings on your computer, not the settings on the web page. Try sending the form from a different computer or changing the address the form is sent to.

The Contact page

The contact page is a simple table with addresses, phone numbers and an e-mail address for Alpe Retreats.

▶ Create a new page based on the template, and save it as Contact.html.

▶ Insert the table then enter the text as shown in the screenshot below.

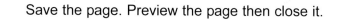

Figure 9.29: The Contact page

▶ Use the E_mail Link icon on the Insert bar to add the e-mail link.

▶ Save the page. Preview the page then close it.

Figure 9.30: Previewing the Contact page

Finishing off

You've now created all the pages in the web site. Now you need to make sure that all the buttons on the nav bar are linked to the correct pages (you'll need to do this in the template). Preview the site in a browser and check all the links. It is possible that pages will appear slightly differently in a browser to how they appear in Design view; if this is the case change the page in Design view so that it looks correct in the browser.

 When you're happy that the whole site works as it should, save and close all the pages.

You've now created a web site! Next we'll focus on how to get your web site online. Don't worry if you don't have any web space at the moment – the next chapter will suggest how to get some free.

Chapter 10
Getting your Web Site Online

You've created a web site but at the moment you can only see it on your computer. This chapter explains how to make your web site accessible to anyone on the Internet.

You can view your web site on your own computer because all the files that make up your web site are stored on your computer. In order that everyone can see your web site, you need to transfer these files onto the server of your Web Host.

The method of transferring files that we will use is called File Transfer Protocol, FTP. Sounds scary – but really it isn't. If you are unsure of what you're doing, just follow the instructions below and you should be OK!

There are three steps to this, which I will cover in more detail in a minute:

 The first step is to make sure that you have access to some web space. If you don't already have any you can sign up for some free web space.

 The second step is to list key pieces of information about your web host account (things like server address – we'll go through this later). You will need this information to enter into Dreamweaver so that when it tries to connect to your web host server it knows where the server is and where your personal directory is on that server.

 The final step is to enter these pieces of information into Dreamweaver. This is really straightforward – you literally just type it in.

If you already have web space

If you already have access to some web space and want to use it for your web site the first thing to do is to find out key information from your web host. To make things easier, the information needed for some popular web host companies (some of which are also ISPs – Internet Service Providers) is listed on the Payne-Gallway web site.

 Go to www.payne-gallway.com/dreamweaver and see if your web host is listed. Note down the information relevant to your web host. There are also other tips on the web site for you to follow if your web host isn't listed.

Signing up for free web space

There are several companies that provide free web space. Any site offering free web hosting will give you on-screen instructions on how to set up the account from their home page. we'll go through how to set up a Portland account as an example.

▶ Go to www.portland.co.uk.

Figure 10.1: The Portland web site

▶ Select Free Web Hosting. This front page may be updated regularly so don't worry if yours looks a bit different. Just look for a link to Free Web Hosting.

▶ Follow the next link to Free Web Hosting.

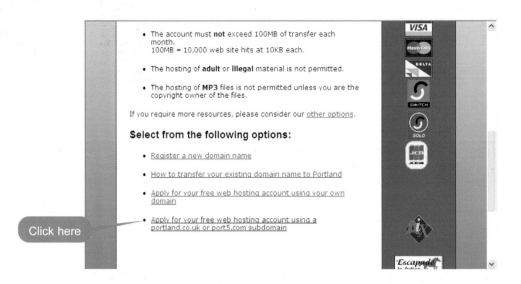

Figure 10.2: The Portland web site

Click on the last link if you don't have a domain name.

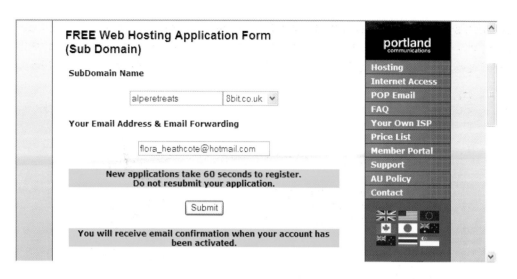

Figure 10.3: The Portland web site

 Now fill out the form. Remember your SubDomain Name – you'll need this later. Click Submit.

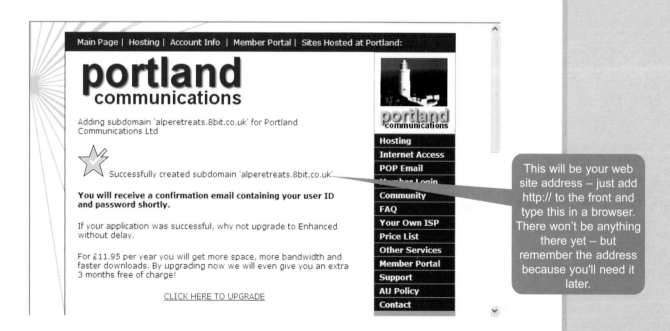

Figure 10.4: The Portland web site

 All done! Now check your e-mail for confirmation that the account has been set up. You will need this e-mail because it contains your user ID and password.

Your web site address will be something like (but not the same as):

http://alperetreats.8bit.com

Now you need to transfer the web page files to the Portland (or other) web server. We'll use Dreamweaver to FTP the files over.

Tip:
It can sometimes take a while for the e-mail to arrive so don't worry if it isn't there straightaway.

Setting up the Remote Info in Dreamweaver

▶ Open Dreamweaver. Select Site, Edit Sites from the menu.

▶ Select Alpe Retreats then click Edit. Under the Advanced tab click Remote Info in the left-hand list.

Figure 10.5: Setting up the Remote Info in the Site Definition window

If you have just signed up for a Portland account

▶ If you have just signed up with Portland, enter the following settings into Dreamweaver:

Access:	FTP
FTP Host:	ftp.portland.co.uk
Host Directory:	(leave blank)
Login:	your User ID – Portland will have e-mailed this to you
Password:	your Password – Portland will have e-mailed this to you

Figure 10.6: Setting up the Remote Info in the Site Definition window

If you are using a different account

▶ Enter the settings listed on the Payne-Gallway web site that are relevant to your web host (go to **www.payne-gallway.co.uk/dreamweaver**). If your web host is not listed on the web site, ask your web host what information needs to be entered into the FTP client.

Does it work?

▶ When you have entered all the information, click the Test button next to the Login field.

Figure 10.7: Connecting to the remote server

Figure 10.8: Connecting to the remote server

If this shows an error, you will need to go back and check all the information you entered. Sometimes if the server is busy it will look like it hasn't worked when really all the information is correct – click the test button a few times just to make sure this isn't the case.

▶ If it has worked you'll get a message saying Connected to Server.

Figure 10.9: Connecting to the remote server

▶ When it looks like it's working, click OK. Click Done in the Edit Sites window.

Cloaking

Before transferring all the files to the server, you need to mark some files that don't need to be transferred. This is called Cloaking. The templates folder doesn't need to be transferred so we'll cloak this now.

▶ First, select Site, Edit Sites from the menu. Select Alpe Retreats then click Edit.

▶ Select Cloaking in the Category list on the left.

▶ Click the Enable Cloaking checkbox.

Figure 10.10: Enabling cloaking

▶ Click OK, then click Done in the Edit Sites window.

▶ Now, in the Site panel right-click the Templates folder.

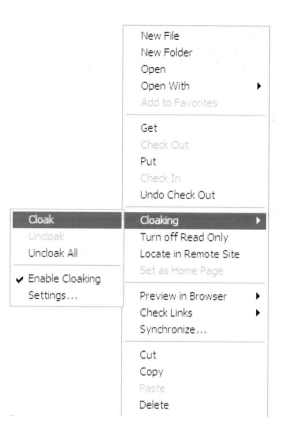

Figure 10.11: Cloaking

Select **Cloaking**, **Cloak** from the context menu.

Figure 10.12: Cloaking

Click **OK** to the message that appears. Notice that the **Templates** folder now has a red line through it.

Figure 10.13: Cloaking

Cloak the **Library** folder in the same way.

Transferring the files

> In the Site panel, click the Expand/Collapse icon.

Figure 10.14: Cloaking

Connecting to the remote host

The remote host is the server that is providing the web space (e.g. Portland).

> Click the Connect to Remote Host icon at the top of the screen.

When connected, you should now see your root directory in the left-hand window. Portland has automatically created a folder called cgi-bin.

Get and Put

Loading files onto the server and removing them is called Get and Put. You need to Put all the files (apart from those you have cloaked) onto the server now.

You can use the Get and Put icons at the top of the screen, but you may prefer to just click and drag the files across.

> Click the index.html file on the right of the screen, and drag it across to the left-hand window. Drop it in the root directory (the top folder).

> You are asked if you want to transfer Dependent files. Click Yes to this – the dependent files needed are basically the image files, but can also include other coding etc. It is safest to include them so you can be sure you have all the required files on the server.

Now we'll transfer all the other files in one go.

> Click the Images folder, hold down the Shift key then click the HTML_files folder. Both folders should now be selected.

Click and hold somewhere in the selection and drag all the files across to the left-hand window. Drop them in the top folder. This time say Yes to include Dependent files.

These files may take a while to upload. When it's done, the files should appear on the left-hand part of the screen. That means that they're on the server!

Your web site is now officially online!

 If you are still connected to the server, click the Disconnect icon. —————

Viewing the web site on the Internet

If you are with Portland, your web site address will be:

http://sitename.port5.com (your sitename will be different)

Your individual web address will be in the e-mail sent to you by Portland.

 Open up a browser window and type the address above, substituting your own site name.

Figure 10.15: Viewing your site online

There it is! Don't worry if your site is not there immediately; some servers will take up to 48 hours to show your web site for the first time (updates won't take this long).

Testing

It is essential to check that all the pages appear as you expect them to.

 Browse through the site, just as you would expect a potential customer to.

Tip:
If you are connected to the server and don't do anything on it for a while, the connection may time-out. If this happens, just reconnect by clicking the **Connect** icon.

Tip:
It is important that you type in **http://sitename. port5.com**, rather than **www.sitename. port5.com**. It won't work otherwise!

Editing pages and uploading them

Making the changes offline

▶ Open the page you want to edit. You must open the file that is on your computer (i.e. on the right-hand window when you expand the site panel, not the file that is on the server).

▶ Save the changes you made.

Uploading the updated pages onto the server

Now you need to Put the file onto the server. This file will overwrite the existing file on the server.

▶ Expand the Site panel. Connect to the server so that you can see all the online files in the left-hand window. Click and drag the updated file from the right of the screen and drop it onto the existing file of the same name in the left of the window.

▶ Click Yes to the prompt about overwriting the existing file. The updated file is now on the server – view it online to check that the changes have been made.

Updating the web site online

If you like, you can connect to the server and open a page that is on the server by double-clicking it in the left-hand pane of the expanded site panel.

By updating a page on the server, you will no longer have the most up-to-date version of the site on your own computer. It's recommended that you keep an up-to-date copy of the site, so that you are not dependent on the server should there be a problem at their end.

Updating the Prices page

The Prices page contains information about the number of places left in each chalet. This means that the Prices page must be regularly updated as the places are taken. To update a page like this you would follow the steps given above – basically make the changes then reload the file back onto the server; the old file will be overwritten by the updated file.

Chapter 11
Frames

Frames are a slightly different way of designing a web site. They can be very useful but they can also cause problems for older browsers and for search engines; for these reasons many web designers choose not to use them.

We'll cover frames briefly so that you know what they are and how to use them.

We'll create a couple of pages from the Alpe Retreats web site using frames – you can go on to complete the whole site if you like.

What are frames?

Basically, frames divide up the browser window into more than one section, and each section displays a different web page. While the user will have gone to one web address, and think they are viewing one web page, they are actually viewing two or more pages. Each section is called a Frame, and the collection of Frames is called a Frameset.

Why is this useful?

A particularly good use of frames is to display the contents or index of a site in one frame, while displaying the currently selected index item in another frame. In the Alpe Retreats web site, we've used a nav bar and a template to ensure the site contents were always visible and each page looked similar; with frames, the nav bar would be a page of its own displayed in a frame, and whatever the user was looking at would be displayed in another frame. Additionally, the Alpe Retreats logo would be on its own on a page, displayed in its own frame.

Creating a new web site

 Using either Windows Explorer or the Site panel in Dreamweaver, create a new folder in the same place as you created the Alpe Retreats Website folder. Name the new folder Alpe Retreats using frames.

Figure 11.1

Tip:
To copy and paste a folder, go to Windows Explorer, select the folder you want to copy by clicking it once, then select **Copy** from the **Edit** menu. Now select the folder you want the other folder to be in and select **Edit, Paste**.

▶ Create the folders shown above, apart from the Images folder.

▶ Copy and paste the Images folder from the original Alpe Retreats site to the new Alpe Retreats using frames site.

▶ In Dreamweaver, select Site, New Site… from the main menu bar.

▶ Click the Advanced tab.

▶ Name the site AlpeRetreats_frames.

▶ Click the Browse icon next to the Local Root Folder field and find the Alpe Retreats using frames folder you have just created.

Figure 11.2: Choosing a local root folder

Your site definition should look like the Figure 11.3.

Figure 11.3: The Site Definition window

▶ Check that the details are correct then click OK.

▶ If it is not already selected, select AlpeRetreats_frames from the drop-down list at the top of the Site panel.

Creating frames

First we will create the Frameset; that is, create a new page and divide it into frames. Next we will insert the nav bar and the Alpe Retreats title graphic into their relevant frames. The pages of the web site that will change as the user goes through the site (the Home page, Resort page etc) will be created separately, then the links will be added to display these pages in a frame. Don't worry about understanding all this – you'll see what happens when you work through the chapter.

Creating the Frameset

Now we'll create a page, divide it into frames then specify which page will appear in each frame.

▶ Open Dreamweaver if it is not already open. A blank page named Untitled-1 should be open.

▶ Select the Frames tab on the Insert bar.

Figure 11.4: The Frames section of the Insert bar

 ▶ Select the frameset second from the right.

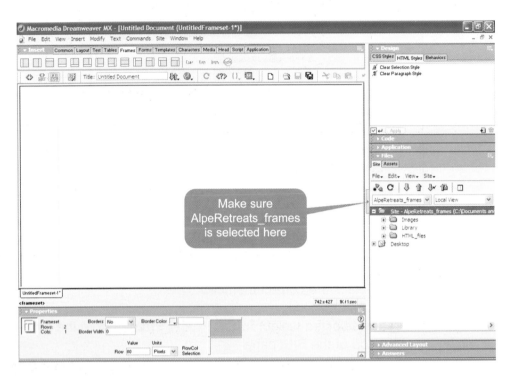

Figure 11.5

Your screen is divided into three frames.

ℹ You can actually get a huge combination of frame patterns by clicking in one of the frames and further dividing it into more frames by clicking another frameset icon. Experiment with this if you like – just select Edit, Undo from the menu when you're done to leave the page looking like the one above.

An alternative method

You can create the same frameset by a different method:

 ▶ Select File, New from the menu.

 ▶ Select Framesets from the left-hand list, and Fixed Top, Nested Left from the right-hand list.

Figure 11.6

▶ Click **Create**. You'll have to delete one of the framesets if you now have two – you only need one.

The Advanced Layout panel

▶ Click the **Frames** panel in the **Advanced Layout** panel group (on the right of the screen),

Figure 11.7: The Frames panel

▶ Click in the **topFrame**.

▶ Rename it in the **Properties** inspector as **titleFrame**. Click **Enter** and the name should change in the **Advanced Layout** panel.

Figure 11.8: Frame properties

▶ Name the other two frames in the same way as navbarFrame and changingFrame.

Figure 11.9: The Frames panel

Tip:
If the name of the frames doesn't update in the **Advanced Layout** panel, it is probably because you didn't press **Enter** after renaming the frame.

Saving the Frameset

The collection of three frames is called a Frameset. You have to save the Frameset separately from the individual frames.

▶ Select File, Save Frameset from the main menu bar.

▶ Enter index.html then save it in the root directory (the Alpe Retreats using Frames directory) and click Save.

Figure 11.10: Saving the Frameset

Saving the frames

As well as saving the Frameset, you have to save each of the three frames.

▶ Select the titleFrame by clicking it in the main window (not by using the Advanced Layout panel).

▶ Select File, Save Frame from the main menu bar.

▶ Enter **title_frame.html** then click **Save**.

Figure 11.11: Saving the title frame

▶ Save the other frames as **navbar_frame.html** and **changing_frame.html**.

Is everything saved?

It can get quite confusing when using frames because you have to name frames, and save them, and then save the frameset! And to make matters worse, if you haven't saved everything you will get error messages when you try and preview the page. One of the simplest ways of making sure everything is saved before previewing a site is to **Save All**.

▶ Right-click on the page tab of the frameset and select **Save All** from the shortcut menu that appears.

The nav bar

First we'll design the frame that contains the nav bar; this will go in the left-hand frame.

▶ Click in the **navbarFrame**

▶ First create a table with **3** rows and **1** column. Once the table is created, convert the width to pixels.

▶ Next, create a nav bar in the centre row of the table you just created. ———

ⓘ The nav bar will be exactly the same as you created in the original Alpe Retreats web site in the template. Be sure to use the images from the correct folder – remember you've got an identical **Images** folder in both the original and new Alpe Retreats sites. Leave the **When Clicked** fields blank for now.

Make sure you select the Use Tables and Insert Vertically options.

Stretch the table vertically so that it covers at least the length of the window. Click and drag the frame border to fit the width of the nav bar. Colour the table background to match the grey in the nav bar.

Figure 11.12

The title frame

Now we'll create the web page containing the title; this will go in the titleFrame.

Click in the titleFrame.

Insert the image AlpeRetreats_logo.jpg.

Figure 11.13

▶ Click and drag the frame borders to resize the frames if you need to. You will probably find that you want to scroll around a frame but that there are no scroll bars – use the arrow keys on your keyboard instead.

▶ Save All and close the frameset for now.

Creating the Home page

The Home page will appear in the changingFrame. The contents of this frame will change between displaying the Home page, the Resort page and the other pages in the site according to what the user has selected on the nav bar.

▶ Create a new blank page and save it as home.html.

▶ Create the home page in just the same way as you did in the original site (except with no template) so that it looks like the page below.

We are a small company that owns and runs four chalets in Val Thorens. For information about the chalets, the resort, prices and booking just follow the links on the left of the screen. If you have any questions please feel free to contact us by phone, fax, post or e-mail

Figure 11.14: The home page

▶ Save and close the page.

Creating the other pages

Now create the other pages in the web site just as you've done the Home page — there should be pages for Resort, Chalets, Prices, Booking and Contact. If you don't have time you don't need to create every page, but you should create at least one to use later on.

Save all the pages and close them.

Selecting the source of each frame

Now you need to specify a source for the changingFrame. Although the contents of this frame will change when the user selects an option from the nav bar, the source you select here is the one that will first appear when a user logs on to your site.

▶ Click in the changingFrame in the Frames panel.

▶ Make sure the home.html file is visible in the Site panel.

▶ Drag the target icon from the Src field in the Properties inspector and drop it on the home.html file in the Site panel.

Figure 11.15: Selecting a source for the changingFrame

The home.html page now appears in the main frame!

Resizing the frames

▷ Click and drag the frame borders so that the title and nav bar fit nicely.

Figure 11.16

▷ Save the frameset then preview the page in a browser.

Figure 11.17: Previewing the Frameset

Creating hyperlinks to open in the changingFrame

▶ Click the Resort button on the nav bar.

▶ Now click on the `<a>` tag at the bottom of the screen so that the button is greyed-out.

Figure 11.18: Selecting the Resort button

▶ In the Properties inspector, drag the target icon onto the Resort.html file in the Site panel.

▶ In the Target field, select changingFrame from the list. This means that the Resort page will open in the changingFrame. If you don't specify a target, the page would open in the same frame as the Resort button, i.e. the navbarFrame.

Figure 11.19: Selecting a Target for the link

▶ Repeat this for the other buttons. You will still need to make a hyperlink for the Home button so that you can return to the home page after viewing other pages.

▶ Save all the frames and the frameset then preview the site in a browser.

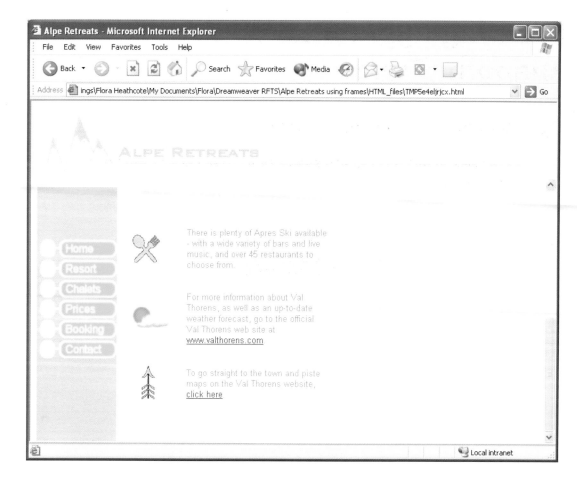

Figure 11.20: Previewing the final site in a browser

The site will feel quite similar to the original site. One of the user-friendly things about using frames is that the title bar and nav bar don't move – in the original site if you scroll down or across a page you can easily lose sight of the title and nav bar.

That's it!

Index